ECO-ANXIETY

Eco-Anxiety

NOLAN
BLACKWOOD

CONTENTS

| 1 |

Introduction

In recent years, a growing number of people have been experiencing heightened anxiety about the environment, the planet, and the potential damage that may be caused as a result of global warming. This anxiety is often intertwined with broader concerns about the future, reflecting a deep-seated worry about the fate of future generations. The consequences of climate change, particularly changes to the environment, may have direct and profound impacts on the physical health of these future generations. As the reality of climate change becomes more widely recognized, there is a burgeoning awareness that people may also experience significant psychological consequences due to global warming, which can adversely affect their mental health.

The Earth has a finite capacity to support human populations and technological advancements without triggering further detrimental consequences. While societal and economic development are crucial, they can lead to the degradation of living conditions, not only by compromising natural resources but also by potentially causing mental health problems. The rapid alteration of the environment and the Earth's atmosphere, driven largely by human-induced emissions of carbon dioxide and other greenhouse gases, is causing widespread shifts in climate patterns. These changes adversely affect weather systems and can lead to events such as rising sea levels, which put increasing numbers of people at risk and undermine food security, leading to severe shortages. The lack of political leadership and the inability of societies with similar democratic institutions and access to the same information about climate change to implement effective policies to slow down the process have been a source of widespread concern among researchers and commentators globally.

Defining Eco-Anxiety

Eco-anxiety is a type of psychological distress linked to concerns about environmental events and their related health outcomes. It is a profound terror that the current destruction of the natural world—the vast and intricate systems that sustain life—is occurring too rapidly for humanity to effectively address. This distress encompasses a wide range of specific anxieties related to climate change and global warming.

Eco-anxiety is broadly defined as "a chronic fear of environmental doom." It represents an existential anxiety about the future of life on Earth, leaving young people of today and tomorrow feeling powerless in the face of the ongoing climate crisis. This unease centers on the risks of experiencing acute stress and helplessness due to the accumulated effects of environmentally unsustainable living, dissonance from feelings of disempowerment despite awareness of environmental impacts, fear of governmental inaction at policy levels, and the threat of a compromised future for young people who will bear the brunt of today's environmental decisions. Consequently, eco-anxiety can play a critical role in initiating and exacerbating stress responses to future concerns about climate change impacts.

Significance of the Topic

This chapter delves into the phenomenon of eco-anxiety, exploring its definition, potential contributing factors, and highlighting the various elements that make it more likely to develop at a young age. It presents notable precursors of the phenomenon and examines possible ways to address eco-anxiety. The phenomenon resonates with children's 'right to be heard' on environmental matters, as enshrined in Article 12 of the Convention on the Rights of the Child (CRC). Religious education in primary schools can offer potential coping mechanisms for eco-anxiety, with approaches that emphasize personal stories, classroom conversations, peer support, inspiration, and creating a 'safe place' to express worries.

Children, like adults, worry about their future. They often wonder what their world will look like when they take on the responsibilities of previous generations. As responsibilities grow, so do their worries. The truth is that the world is changing, largely for environmental reasons, and an alarming number of children are concerned about various environmental problems. These children, who fear for the future of our world and the life chances of future generations, are experiencing what has been described as eco-anxiety. This book argues that eco-anxiety should not be viewed as an unusual individual problem but rather as an understandable response to the ongoing global ecological crisis.

| 2 |

Understanding Environmental Concerns

In times of disaster, we often hear concerns about the perceived inefficiency and incompetence of government agencies in managing public safety. People's beliefs about government effectiveness and leadership become critical in crisis communication, a situation exacerbated by the shifting messages emerging from the post-truth environment. Advocates of disaster capitalism may seek to erode trust in state-run services, aiming to justify their privatization to the public. This distrust, combined with the feelings of loss and invasiveness, raises psychological tension about mass disasters and the relationship between government and enterprise-environment interactions. This tension contributes to feelings of hopelessness in the face of destructive actions taken in the name of progress, such as mass environmental clearances in preparation for mitigating or adapting to climate change-induced disasters.

Types of Environmental Concerns

What kind of environmental concerns are currently on people's minds? Scholars refer to a basic set of framings for public concern as 'theories of concern'. These theories suggest that most people view environmental issues as related to the loss of nature, excessive pollution, and overconsumption. Psychologically, this pertains to our relationship with nature, often rooted in what we perceive as our cherished places and nature's beauty. Abstractly, it involves the loss of ecosystem services or natural capital. It's about our sense of community living and our instinctive desire to protect them. In essence, nature is deemed beneficial in many ways, and its loss is particularly troubling when caused by human actions.

Another facet of these psychological concerns, especially with repetitive messaging about doom and disaster, is the perceived inability to address such dire consequences even if we desire to. This relates to concerns about efficacy or feelings of hopelessness. The prevalence of doom-laden narratives in environmental campaigns suggests that such strategies have long been used to galvanize public concern. 'Doom-mongering' as a rational strategy to raise public awareness has become a common conception of environmentalism, supported by scientific projections of potential annihilation.

Global Climate Change

The significant changes resulting from climate change create profound social and personal uncertainty and stress. The fear of losing something precious and confronting potential life-threatening situations leads to ecological anxiety. Individuals often feel they have little control over their actions, decisions, and life conditions, exacerbating this existential concern known as eco-anxiety. As active agents within natural and social environments, humans are deeply affected by the negative emotions arising from global environmental changes. Consequently, unresolved personal worries and an increased sense of urgency can lead to negative consequences for personal well-being, necessitating effective coping strategies to address the progression of crises and prevent mental illness.

Undoubtedly, global climate change plays a critical role in driving significant ecological transformations across the Earth's biotic systems. Future climate change is predicted to cause substantial shifts in species distribution and interaction, affecting both short-term and long-term ecosystem functions. These changes will be particularly pronounced further away from the poles, posing adaptation challenges for many organisms. On a global scale, climate change will also impact habitats and water availability, increase the frequency and severity of natural disasters, and intensify food stressors for a growing human population. The consequences of climate change extend to human systems, influencing public health, socioeconomic conditions, culture, and international conflicts.

Biodiversity Loss

The threat of losing various species due to human activity intensifies anxiety, fear, panic, sadness, and profound emotional pain. Coping strategies are essential for managing these feelings. Some suggest learning coping skills such as the Five Practices of Well-Being proposed by students from St. Michael's College, which include exercising and eating healthily, engaging in deep conversations, grounding oneself through actions that help others, engaging in relaxing activities like meditation and journaling, reconnecting with nature, and maintaining boundaries against an 'all or nothing' mindset in activism.

Biodiversity loss is a crucial aspect of climate anxiety. According to the International Union for Conservation of Nature (IUCN) Red List, significant percentages of amphibians, mammals, birds, and marine mammals are now threatened with extinction. For instance, oceanic dolphin populations have the lowest genetic diversity among higher animals, impacting their adaptability to human-induced pressures. The Living Planet Index indicates that vertebrate population sizes have declined by 68% since 1970. While some declines in the Global North might be mitigated through technological and biotechnological advancements and increased species protection, these statistics offer no cause for celebration. The large-scale reduction in biodiversity has extensive cultural, spiritual, ethical, and policy implications, such as diminishing opportunities for recreation and tourism and depriving humans of essential ecosystem services. Disconnection from nature can lead to a loss of empathy for environmental issues, further exacerbating the crisis.

| 3 |

The Psychological Impact of Environmental Concerns

In 1997, a significant study found that a group of 1,200 people were suffering from symptoms of eco-anxiety. Most individuals in the study reported being diagnosed with depression, 20% felt it was highly likely they were experiencing despair, and only 5% believed despair was unlikely. Witnesses to the consequences of global warming are predicted to suffer from anxiety, depression, PTSD, and increased rates of aggression toward themselves and others. These mental health issues may particularly affect members of environmental NGOs, as voluntary factors are positively related to a higher mental health burden. There is evidence that living near visible reminders of the consequences of global warming can affect mental health. For example, communities in the Arctic have experienced mental health problems following the loss of their livelihoods and declining living standards as direct consequences of climate change.

Research on the psychological impact of the current environmental situation is limited. However, existing studies suggest that people are experiencing significant negative psychological reactions. The potential for personal suffering is amplified by the multifaceted nature of these reactions. They include fears for their future, their family's future, fear for the entire planet, an awareness of their disempowerment, anger because they feel unheard, guilt about the suffering of others, and grief for a planet being ravaged. These complex emotions make it difficult for individuals to cope, leading to a tendency to distance themselves from nature and prioritize other immediate concerns.

Eco-Anxiety: Definition and Symptoms

Eco-anxiety is defined as a type of anxiety caused by serious concerns about the future of the ecosystem. This includes fears of a polluted planet, contaminated air, land, and oceans, dead regions, or areas unnaturally affected by human activities, and the worst effects of global climate change. Children and young people may express eco-anxiety in various ways, from vigorous, even aggressive expressions, to burying their concerns, which may seep out as varying degrees of anxiety, from vague uneasiness to full-fledged panic attacks. Although eco-anxiety is not yet an official diagnostic category in the Diagnostic and Statistical Manual of Mental Disorders (DSM-5), psychiatric professionals describe symptoms such as irritability, sleeplessness, and traumatic symptoms.

Children often think and worry about current and future issues impacting the world. They understand that environmental problems will not resolve themselves and that the world may suffer from a shortage of resources. With clear explanations and conversations, children can comprehend the causes and severity of eco-anxiety, which poses a significant threat to environmental education. Excessive anxiety and fear can hinder their ability to understand new ideas about the environment.

As climate change and various environmental issues increasingly impact lives around the world, it is not surprising that eco-anxiety has gained attention. Researchers, children's book authors, and teachers are introducing children to this new type of anxiety, stemming from news about melting ice caps, declining animal populations, and extreme weather events.

Prevalence and Risk Factors

Globally, adverse effects experienced from rapidly developing ecological precursors include social disorganization, conflicts, grief over species loss, and the loss of a peaceful living environment. These impacts are of concern to nursing and mental health professionals. Related literature has led to the recognition of a subclinical syndrome known as eco-anxiety, characterized by symptoms such as mood swings, burnout, impotence, restlessness, insomnia, irritability, depressive symptoms, increased suicidal tendencies, crying, overeating, excessive concern, denial, and loss of confidence in the future.

Encouraging reliable prevalence data is challenging due to the lack of clear diagnostic criteria. Prevalence estimates for state-based symptoms range from 16 to 46% of adolescents and 17 to 38% of young adults. A study found that 40% of a sample of Australian adolescents reported feeling "particularly anxious about climate change and its impact." Some individuals report symptoms consistent with a nervosa spectrum disorder when thinking about climate change, but this should be interpreted cautiously and not seen as a general prevalence estimate for eco-anxiety.

| 4 |

Coping Strategies for Eco-Anxiety

Individual Coping Mechanisms
When individuals find themselves increasingly affected by anxiety or emotional distress about the future of the planet and its inhabitants, it's natural to seek strategies to reduce these negative feelings. This section explores several strategies that may help individuals continue to be proactive in their engagement with sustainability issues while also improving their well-being.

Psychological research into individual coping mechanisms for environmental concerns often highlights strategies that soothe symptoms without necessarily addressing the core problem. Many people use distancing as a coping mechanism, such as visiting nature to assuage their concerns. Consumption is also popular—buying products as a means of coping is a common response, although it can sometimes be unreflective and combined with other behaviors like conserving water or turning off lights. However, this pattern of consumption, while comforting in the short term, can have significant negative environmental impacts.

Engaging in eco-therapeutic activities—leisure and recreation in nature—can foster pro-environmental values, abilities, and well-being. For example, studies indicate that children who spend more time in nature demonstrate greater interest, empathy, and respect for the environment. High-quality nature activities are associated with increased long-term health and well-being, as found in research involving Finnish and Canadian children. Additionally, individuals who use natural environments for stress reduction and restoration tend to score higher on environmental well-being scales, as noted by Kaplan and Talbot.

Community and Collective Actions

Involvement in environmental organizations provides significant benefits for landowner well-being, offering a sense of purpose, personal growth, and relief from emotional fatigue. Volunteering can help alleviate feelings of helplessness, leading to a sense of achievement, excitement, life satisfaction, and good health. Successful community involvement often leads to feelings of connectedness, empowerment, and satisfaction.

There is also a group of pioneers and practitioners who adopt political and associative forms of action to combat environmental problems, such as collective or legislative actions promoting environmental responsibility and local well-being. Strengthening local communities helps prevent isolated and atomized citizens from turning to extremist movements or xenophobic positions.

Awareness of broader environmental changes, combined with engagement in relevant community-level actions, helps some people manage feelings of eco-anxiety. Preserving local environments and landscapes is important for mood and well-being, offering balance in life and acting as a helpful antidote to pre-existing eco-anxiety or other mental health problems. Community and collective action, such as involvement in local environmental organizations, community associations, and volunteering, can increase a sense of purpose, well-being, and connectedness. Efforts to influence decisions by state institutions, and associated direct or practical actions, are seen as useful and attainable in one's place of residence or community. Small-scale actions, which are visible on a day-to-day basis, engage participants more easily than large-scale and remote issues.

| 5 |

Building Resilience in the Face of Environmental C

By cultivating hope, individuals maintain the necessary energy and motivation to engage in positive actions. Relationships with adults who model constructive coping strategies, including working through difficult issues productively, are key for building resiliency. Schools, religious and spiritual communities, clubs, and other organizations play important roles, with special care taken to open diverse cultural pathways and explore multiple ways of knowing and doing in this process. Parents, guardians, and other caring adults should be vigilant for signs of chronic fear and hopelessness in young people related to climate change anxiety and build practices to address these patterns early on.

Resilience is expressed in diverse ways, depending on individual values and the family, community, and cultural environments. It is not a fixed state but an evolving set of capacities that help individuals and communities contend with, cope with, and manage change. Importantly, resilience can be developed and nurtured, and developmental experiences can help buffer stress. Youth involved in structured and meaningful extracurricular activities or oriented toward action in response to environmental problems often develop feelings of efficacy and tools to work through feelings of despair and hopelessness.

Resilience is the ability to maintain a stable equilibrium in the face of physical, emotional, environmental, and social stressors. However, not everyone demonstrates resilience in adversity. Resilience and adaptation are influenced by various factors, including socioeconomic status, social connectedness, and access to cultural and material resources.

Psychological Resilience

Rather than focusing on mental health illness and treatment, the development of conservation psychologies should aim to understand how humans can maintain healthy states of mind despite the current environmental crisis. Neurological research provides data on how various biological systems operate in healthy states, which can help develop these conservation psychologies. For example, cognition associated with a happy state of mind helps animals establish long-term cooperative social bonds.

Historically, researchers have focused on how individuals can adapt personality traits or abilities to increase resilience by, for example, learning to become more optimistic. The mindfulness movement suggests that training people to be more mindful might increase psychological resilience. By focusing on the present and avoiding cognitive traps of the past or future, external life events might have less impact on mental well-being. This could reduce pressures on healthcare systems and demands on social services. The effectiveness of these methods depends on social processes and brain regulation mechanisms.

Cultivating Hope and Agency

Calling attention to the historically constructed nature of environmental attitudes can provide clues on cultivating hope and agency in relation to the environment. Environmental psychologists are knowledgeable about empirical studies documenting what helps and hampers positive environmental behaviors. The ways we present environmental goals and behaviors matter, as historically constructed attitudes may harbor resources that help ameliorate perceptions of climate change leading to anxiety.

Eco-anxiety often arises from a sense of helplessness due to the vastness of environmental problems and the perceived inability to exert influence. Tackling eco-anxiety requires resources that cultivate hope and agency, key tools for clinical and educational psychologists to equip their clients and students with. Summaries of positive stories and lifestyle changes that have improved mental well-being are effective yet under-utilized resources for clinicians. Teaching strategies to help students cultivate hope and a sense of agency include goal-setting, visualization of positive futures, identification of simple practices that stimulate well-being, and fostering a sense of connection to the nonhuman world.

| 6 |

Educational and Advocacy Initiatives

R esearch has shown that many people feel paralyzed in response to the reality of climate change. Addressing the emotional and rational aspects of this knowledge is crucial for moving from engagement to empowerment. Educational and advocacy efforts focus on creating safe spaces for dialogue among students, peers, and teachers about the environmental challenges the world faces. These spaces should be positive and hopeful, providing support and guidance rather than debating the existence of environmental issues. Eco-anxious students seek understanding and actionable solutions to the problems they recognize.

Educational and advocacy organizations have intensified their initiatives to combat the climate eco-anxiety that students experience. These efforts aim to inform students about the impacts of climate change and provide actionable advice for daily life, delivered in a hopeful, constructive, and proactive manner to counteract feelings of helplessness and stress that often accompany climate knowledge.

Environmental Education Programs

We need to develop educational initiatives that build engagement with the environment to conserve it for future generations, empower individuals to improve their quality of life, and enhance capacity for action, ultimately boosting personal well-being. Starting with programs that educate is essential, but we must also develop capabilities for recognizing broader factors influencing decisions about environmental resilience. This includes reflecting on worldviews, power, and developing competencies in advocacy and negotiation, and understanding the effectiveness of actions. Addressing vast environmental concerns should shift from one-off projects to expressing shared meanings across society.

Environmental educational programs (EEDs) are people-centered and participatory processes that help communities develop sustainability for quality living environments now and in the future. These programs may include formal education (curricula and classes) or informal educational processes addressing local sustainability needs. A review of over 700 programs in more than 90 countries revealed three key outcomes: increased knowledge and appreciation of the environment, more pro-environmental behaviors aligned with sustainable development, and the ability to conserve both environmental resources and quality of life in a region.

Advocacy and Activism

Optimism alone can be dangerous, leading to ineffectual behavior. Therefore, communities should balance passion and empathy. Advocates and activists must make time for education, self-awareness, and self-care. These actions can nurture anger and distress, enabling greater social and environmental awareness and stimulating higher personal responsibility. By doing so, advocates and activists become better prepared, organized, and capable of managing future actions and community interactions.

Communities committed to educational activities contribute to alternative values common to a sustainable, pluralistic, diverse, empathetic, and equal society. Engaging in innovative and creative community interactions and actions can be a key source of satisfaction and emotional stability during stressful times. Taking a stand or getting involved through activism and advocacy can provide a sense of purpose, strengthen the community, and contribute positively. These actions can reduce anxiety, foster positive feelings of hope about future change, and renew a sense of vigor and pride.

Advocates and activists should, however, ensure they make time for self-care to maintain their effectiveness and well-being.

| 7 |

Policy Implications and Recommendations

Addressing anxiety is crucial for strengthening the relationship between general anxiety reduction and environmental policy. In American society, ecological concerns are often viewed as a liberal priority. In a post-carbon world, mindfulness, self-regulation, managing motivational affect, and practicing new habits become personal tasks relevant to anxiety reduction. These strategies also represent opportunities that modern market capitalism seeks to harness. Given the challenges of climate change, resource depletion, and human psychological numbing, we must be vigilant about these strategies. Environmental and climate policy requires a conscious and strategic approach to manage these opportunities effectively.

With growing research on eco-anxiety and its connections to other psychological phenomena, it is evident that policies addressing environmental crises, dangers, and threats offer opportunities to prevent and reduce harms associated with emotional repercussions, such as eco-anxiety. Engagement with environmental concerns can be a significant growth opportunity for individual climate coping, provided the requisite psychological and moral support is available. Certain policy changes can foster both long-term and short-term growth in psychological resilience, social connectivity, and emotional autonomy. Other measures can create space for individuals and communities to address their eco-anxiety in their ways.

Governmental Policies and Regulations

Feelings of empowerment build self-confidence. Moving from conversations about contemplating solutions to discussing meaningful government participation and access can positively impact mental health. Studies show that increased awareness of environmental issues reduces emotional worries. Publicly engaging with environmental issues within individuals' control can open up possibilities for public discussion and participation. People often feel pleased when directly involved in solving problems.

Policies and regulations can support individuals in coping with environmental anxieties. Regulations ordering psychological protection for workers in high-stress areas suggest the importance of support in these fields. Individuals excessively worried can seek support from psychotherapists.

Most people participate in environmental solutions promoted by governments and regulatory bodies. Ordinary citizens calling upon their governments to support change can be empowering, calming, and beneficial for mental health. Identifying and undertaking tasks that improve the local environment can help individuals feel in control of their surroundings and reduce eco-anxiety. This can also help young people manage feelings of melancholy and depression regarding their future and specific threats they perceive.

International Agreements and Treaties

The international legal community plays a critical role in recognizing global responsibility to future generations through developing international norms of environmental protection.

General and specific principles on protecting human interests from environmental harms have been internationalized by inter-state practice through customary international law, permitting certain forms of intervention and response to activities affecting the global commons. One notable agreement is the Montreal Protocol of 1987, addressing substances that deplete the ozone layer.

International action on environmental problems began with the United Nations Conference on the Human Environment in Stockholm in 1972. This conference led to the creation of the United Nations Environment Program (UNEP) to oversee global environmental developments and keep the world informed. By the end of the decade following Stockholm, several agreements and protocols were established, such as the Convention on International Trade in Endangered Species (CITES), The Ramsar Convention on migratory birds, The Bonn Agreement, and The London Convention on the Prevention of Marine Pollution. These agreements drew government attention to environmental problems and the damage to human health and food chains. While not global, these agreements, referred to by Swedish Prime Minister Olof Palme as "small torches in the darkness," demonstrated the potential for legal cooperation.

| 8 |

Conclusion

The main focus of this book has been to familiarize environmental researchers with the concepts of eco-anxiety, nature relatedness, and biophilia, clearly outlining their significance and presenting testimonials from especially vulnerable individuals. Our goal was to highlight an important gap in this growing field and emphasize the need for new research related to eco-anxiety concerns. While environmental problems have long been recognized and studied, recent efforts to cope with climate change must place greater emphasis on the far-reaching consequences for the mental health of the population.

The related concepts of nature relatedness and the eco-anxiety model provide a robust foundation based on rigorous research, going beyond mere organic appreciation to address profound psychological impacts. Widespread adoption of these concepts can significantly advance academic research, clinical practice, and public policy implementation. They have the potential to influence the impact and direction of current intervention practices at both individual and societal levels, offering long-term emotional health benefits. Recognizing the true shore on which we stand may be the most important step in providing help to control eco-anxiety.

We presented an eco-anxiety trigger model based on environmental and psychological impacts, leading to the need to design interventions addressing eco-anxiety at these levels. The main focus was on the psychological impact of eco-anxiety and associated concepts, identifying the potential mental health hazards related to environmental anxieties. We explored theories connecting nature relatedness, emotional affinity, and biophilia, outlining a vulnerability stress approach model where nature relatedness intersects with complex environmental problems, potentially overwhelming emotionally sensitive individuals and transitioning them to a mentally exhausting state of eco-anxiety.

Summary of Key Points

- **Retreating**: Taking a break from usual environmental activities to relax and recharge.
- **Learning**: Expanding knowledge about nature, the planet, and human impact.
- **Meditating**: Using meditation to manage stress and clear the mind for effective action.
- **Participating**: Engaging in community efforts, such as waste collection days or activist groups, to address eco-concerns.

Eco-anxiety is an overwhelming sense of worry or panic due to environmental concerns, first used to describe individuals grieving the loss of ecosystems and fearing the future. Though not a unique psychiatric condition, eco-anxiety is recognized by governments and health organizations as a significant mental health risk, affecting children, adults, and pregnant women. Eco-anxious individuals often feel compelled to make eco-friendly decisions in their daily lives to protect the environment. The key is developing strategies to better cope with these environmental concerns.

Future Directions for Research and Practice

Currently, knowledge and understanding of eco-anxiety are limited but rapidly growing. Insufficient empirical data exists to confirm or disconfirm proposed accounts of eco-anxiety, leading to hypothetical typologies and potential measurement errors. Detailed pictures of eco-anxiety, such as its main perpetrators, prevalence, and common exacerbatory stressors, remain unclear.

- **Quantitative and Mixed-Methods Research**: Address the nature of eco-anxiety, variables that precede, accompany, or follow eco-anxiety, and its real and perceived impacts. Research should also focus on ameliorating eco-anxiety and its symptoms and possibilities for proactive engagement with related threats and risks in the 21st century.

Advancing the empirical basis and practice of eco-anxiety and related constructs requires additional research, both quantitative and qualitative, within these categories. This will provide a more detailed understanding of eco-anxiety, its impacts, and effective intervention strategies, ultimately contributing to better mental health outcomes in the face of environmental challenges.